Sandra Markle
Snow School

Illustrated by
Alan Marks

ini **Charlesbridge**

With love for my children, Scott and Holly Markle—S. M.

To Lucia, Cecilia, Solly, and Gabriel—A. M.

Acknowledgments
The author would like to thank Dr. Tom McCarthy, executive director of Snow Leopard Programs for Panthera, an organization dedicated to ensuring the future of wild cats. A special thank-you to Skip Jeffery for his support during the creative process.

Published by Charlesbridge
85 Main Street
Watertown, MA 02472
(617) 926-0329
www.charlesbridge.com

Library of Congress Cataloging-in-Publication Data
Markle, Sandra.
    Snow school / Sandra Markle ; illustrated by Alan Marks.
        p. cm.
    Includes bibliographical references.
    ISBN 978-1-58089-410-4 (reinforced for library use)
1. Snow leopard—Juvenile literature. 2. Snow leopard—Infancy—Juvenile literature.
3. Learning in animals—Juvenile literature. I. Marks, Alan, 1957– ill. II. Title.
QL737.C23M2735 2013
599.75'55—dc23   2012000790

Printed in the United States of America
(hc) 10 9 8 7 6 5 4 3 2

Illustrations done in watercolor and pencil on Fabriano 5 paper
Display type set in Elroy, designed by Christian Schwartz for Monotype Imaging
Text type set in Fairfield by Monotype Imaging
Color separations by KHL Chroma Graphics, Singapore
Printed January 2014 by Worzalla Publishing Company in Stevens Point, Wisconsin, USA
Production supervision by Brian G. Walker
Designed by Martha MacLeod Sikkema

It's May—springtime in Pakistan's Hindu Kush Mountains.
But high up on gravel-strewn slopes,
where only the hardiest plants grow,
snowflakes still dance in the icy wind.
Inside a den, week-old snow leopard cubs—
a brother and sister—
wait for their mother's return.

While his sister yowls to be fed, the male peeks outside
with newly opened eyes, spies the snowflakes,
and crawls out to explore.

Suddenly a golden eagle swoops down, with talons thrust out.
The mother snow leopard arrives just in time.
Growling and swatting, she drives the eagle away.
Then she picks up the cub in gentle jaws
and carries him into the den.
So the little male learns his first lesson.
Outside the den, it's a dangerous world.

Five weeks old and nearly double his birth weight,
the little male is a fuzzy ball of muscle and curiosity.
He sneaks up on the twitching tip of his mother's long tail.

Then his sister pounces on him.
The pair tumbles, swatting and biting whatever they can reach.
This way they build strong muscles and practice hunting skills.
Mother ends the training session with tongue licks.
When she flops down, the cubs snuggle against her
to nurse and nap.

At two months old, the cubs are nearly five times their birth weight.
They're shedding baby teeth for adult teeth—all pointed and sharp.

One day their mother arrives, dragging an ibex she's killed.
The pair attack this prey, biting the ears—the only part
thin enough to fit in their young mouths.
Mother tears open the belly, and the cubs nose in,
discovering the smell and taste
of what they'll one day catch for themselves—
if they learn their lessons.

At five months old, the cubs look like small adults and eat a lot.
Mother hunts every morning and evening to bring home food.
But one afternoon, she calls the cubs with throaty chuffs.
They leave the den behind to go hunting with her.

In their smoky gray, black-spotted coats,
the three snow leopards look like shadows slipping over rocks.
The cubs mimic their mother when she stops
to rub her cheek on a boulder—another lesson.
Always leave your scent to claim your favorite hunting places.

Mother and cubs climb on big paws
to the crest of giant sloping slabs of rock.
Far below, a cluster of ibex munches grass and twigs.
Crouched low, eyes fixed on her target, the mother snow leopard
steps carefully so no pebbles fall—and no ibex notice.
Trailing after their mother, the male cub squeezes past his sister.
She attacks. They wrestle. Loose stones tumble, clattering downhill.
Ibex scatter—running, leaping, escaping.
Empty stomachs make this lesson one the cubs won't forget.
Be quiet when you go hunting.

The snow leopards nap, curled up together against the cold wind.
When the full moon rises, they go hunting again.
This time when prey is close, mother chuffs
and the cubs stop to watch.

The female snow leopard sneaks up on the grazing ibex.
They flee. She chases one that lags behind.
This ibex runs fast downhill, leaping, twisting, turning.
The cat charges after it—stays balanced—and pounces.
Sharing their mother's meal reinforces today's lesson.
Be quick and stay on your feet to catch fast food.

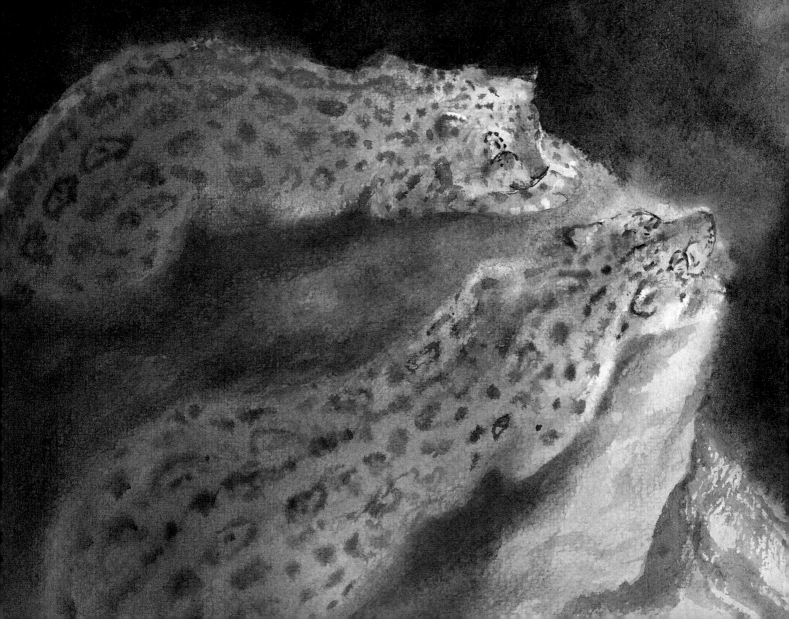

Sometimes, while their mother sleeps, the cubs chase each other.
Twisting and turning in hot pursuit,
both winner and loser gain from these training sessions.
The cubs grow stronger, faster, bolder, and able to land on target—
even if the prey is only a snarling brother or sister.

One day while their mother sleeps, the young male hunts a pika.
He mimics his mother's sneak and charge.
When the pika flees, the cub pounces—and makes his first kill.

When his sister arrives, he chases her away.
But while he's gone, ravens swoop down and steal the pika.
Losing his prey teaches the young hunter a hard lesson.
Always guard your food until you're finished eating.

Nights grow longer, and days remain cold.
Snowflakes fall and stay.
One day icy winds blast, biting bare noses and whipping snow
into a blinding white fog.
Mother leads the cubs into a den among jumbled boulders.
Safe there, the trio curls up in a warm heap to sleep
while the blizzard rages outside.
This way the cubs learn a lifesaving lesson.
Always find shelter from a storm.

When one storm follows another,
drifting snow covers scarce plants,
and ibex move down the mountain to graze.
The snow leopards follow their prey all the way to the valley.
There the snow is deeper, making chasing prey harder—
but at least there's prey to hunt.

One morning the cats come close to a flock of sheep
tended by humans.
The hungry cubs crouch, but their mother quietly pads away,
teaching another lesson.
No matter what, stay clear of humans.

That night, mother kills an old markhor too weak to run fast.

But just as the family starts to eat,

six wolves trot up, snarling and flashing sharp teeth.

Outnumbered by these predators, mother quickly leads the cubs away.

The cubs will never forget this lesson.

Staying safe is more important than having a full stomach.

All winter long, the snow leopard cubs live mainly
on what their mother can catch.
But sometimes, they help feed themselves by hunting small prey,
like marmots, pikas, or snowcocks.

At last, spring sunshine warms the air and melts most of the snow.
Then the cats track the grazers back up the rugged slopes
to claim their high mountain hunting range.

All spring and summer, the cubs follow their mother,
sharing the prey she kills
while they grow bigger and stronger.

Then one summer night, the young male snow leopard
is the first to pick up the scent of ibex.
The grazers don't see this moon shadow spring to life
until the hunter is charging straight at them
down the gravel slope.
The young male chooses just one ibex—runs fast—and pounces.

The young male snow leopard has completed his lessons.
His sister and mother share his first big kill.
The male will soon leave his mother.
Before long, his sister will leave, too.
The lessons their mother taught them will help
the young snow leopards survive,
hunting alone in their rugged home.

Snow Leopards Are Amazing!

There may be as few as 3,500 snow leopards living wild and free in the world today. An adult is about as big as an adult German shepherd and able to catch prey that outweighs it by nearly three times. Snow leopards live and hunt in some of the world's highest and most rugged mountains, in South and Central Asia. Snow leopards have special features that help them thrive in this unique habitat.

❉ They have thick fur and small, rounded ears to reduce heat loss. They also have extra-large nasal cavities to warm and moisten the cold, dry air they breathe.

❉ Snow leopards have big feet. These act like snowshoes to spread out their weight and keep them from sinking into deep snow. Hair on the bottom of their feet and between their toes improves their grip on ice and slick rocks.

❉ Their short front legs and longer, muscular back legs let snow leopards successfully make super-long leaps—jumping several times their body length. Their thick tail, which stretches out nearly as long as their body, helps them balance while running and jumping.

Find Out More

To find out even more about snow leopards, check out these sources:

Johnston, Marianne. *Snow Leopards and Their Babies* (Zoo Life Book). New York: PowerKids Press, 1999. Get up close to snow leopards living in zoos and learn about this rare cat's behavior.

Landau, Elaine. *Snow Leopards: Hunters of the Snow and Ice* (Animals of the Snow and Ice). Berkley Heights, NJ: Enslow, 2010.

Planet Earth: Mountains: Snow Leopard Hunt
http://dsc.discovery.com/videos/planet-earth-mountains-snow-leopard-hunt.html
Follow a female snow leopard as she visits her year-old cub and hunts.

Snow Leopard Twins
http://whyevolutionistrue.wordpress.com/2009/09/05/caturday-felids-snow-leopard-twins/
See snow leopard twin cubs explore and play together. These videos are too cute to miss.

Author's Note

Without a doubt, wild big cats are among the most fascinating animals on earth—and none more so than the snow leopard. That cat is so difficult to observe in its rugged mountain home that there are still many unanswered questions about its life and behavior. For me, writing a story about a real animal first involves getting to know my subject well by studying it in every way possible, including, when I can, observing the real animal in action. While I couldn't climb the high mountains to search for snow leopards, I was thrilled to be able to watch films supplied by people who did, and to talk to Dr. Tom McCarthy about his snow leopard research. He's spent many years studying snow leopards in the wild and working to help protect these cats. You can watch snow leopards in action, too, via the video links I've provided. To learn even more about snow leopards and how your family can contribute to the effort to help protect these cats in their wild homes, visit the following websites: Panthera: Leaders in Wild Cat Conservation (http://www.panthera.org/species/snow-leopard) and Snow Leopard Trust (http://www.snowleopardtrustuk.org/snow-leopards.htm).